Trade Marks Made Easy

How to Register a Trademark
in the UK and Europe
Without Using a Lawyer
and Save Yourself £100s

Gary Jennings

Trade Marks Made Easy

How to Register a Trademark
in the UK and Europe
Without Using a Lawyer
and Save Yourself £100s

Published by GJ International Ltd
www.gj-intl.com
PO Box 88, Bodmin. PL30 3WZ. UK

ISBN 978-0-9559333-2-5

Cover design and logo design by www.juicymarketing.co

Rules of Don't ®, and the 'Trade Marks Made Easy logo' are registered Trade Marks of GJ International Ltd.

www.TradeMarksMadeEasy.com

Disclaimer

This book is dedicated:

To everyone who has helped me get to where I am today…

…to everyone who has tried to get in my way and failed…

…and to all those people who looked at the dedication page of my first book and asked "why didn't you include me?"…it's for all of you too.

But most of all, to Diane. For ever, for always x

CONTENTS

INTRODUCTION

A few years ago I was copied by a competitor and there was absolutely nothing I could do about it. I lost business, market share, customers and money. I didn't want it to happen again and researched various ways to protect everything I had built up for the future. I found I could protect myself and my business from being copied by registering Trade Marks.

I used a Trade Mark lawyer to conduct my first two registrations; I thought it was the only way to do it. I gave him all the information; he made the application, but I still had to understand the requirements in order to instruct him and answer his questions.
I am not a lawyer or a Trade Mark attorney; I run my own small business and every part is precious to me, so I really wanted to understand and get it right, and in the process I also found some really useful information.

In looking into Trade Marks a little deeper, I discovered the Right Start Service which is designed to enable you to apply for your own UK Trade Mark registration without using a lawyer. For my next two Trade Marks I researched information and used the Right Start Service, saving time and cost (about 80% cheaper than using a lawyer). I did make mistakes, and then learnt how to overcome them.

Even though the Right Start Service is a straight forward system, I needed to understand the process, the requirements and what it takes to be successful. Each part of applying for my own Trade Mark raised more questions and so I researched the answers. There is a lot of legal jargon and legislation out there, but I could not find one simple source that could explain what I needed to know, at the level I needed, and not blow my mind...so I decided to write about what I have learnt and done to help other people avoid the confusion and register their own Trade Marks with confidence.

This book gives you ALL the questions I had along the way, and the answers I found. I even tell you about the conversations I have had with Trade Mark examiners on how they assess applications. It's not a legal manual, it's a simple, quick, bite-sized practical way of what you need to know, what you need to check, and what you need to prepare so you can apply for your own Trade Marks and protect your business, your brand, your future.

There is no smoke and mirrors; you get the benefit of my hindsight and experiences of how to Trade Mark.

The interesting thing is that once I knew how to register a Trade Mark in the UK, I was also able to register Trade Marks throughout the European Union; all this information is in this book too.

I've spoken with many Trade Mark lawyers, who agree that the Right Start Service is a positive step for individuals and companies alike to protect their business. They have seen their business shift towards more complicated issues such as making and defending oppositions and registering complicated marks. In cases such as these I would definitely seek advice from the legal profession, but for all my 'ordinary' marks for names, words, hook-lines or logos I always do it myself, stay in control and save myself literally £100s in legal fees. You don't have to be a business or an organisation to register a Trade Mark, you can also apply in your own name.

The great thing is now I have registered Trade Marks, I have all the legal rights of protection in the UK and/or EU, and I can now stop anyone trying to rip me off, copy me, or jump on my bandwagon. If I can protect my business and my brand this way, and my future revenues, you can too.

CAN I REALLY REGISTER A TRADE MARK MYSELF IN THE UK?

In the UK, Trade Mark applications are made to the Intellectual Property Office (IPO), who are responsible for all types of Intellectual Property registration, including Patents, Trade Marks and Design Registrations.

Registering a Trade Mark in the UK can be achieved by using the services of a Trade Mark professional, or you can register the Trade Mark yourself.

You do not need to be a Limited Company to own a registered Trade Mark. Anyone who needs to protect their distinctive brand and/or name can register a Trade Mark whether they are a charity, partnership, sole trader or an individual.

The IPO has many services; the Right Start Service is a system for registering Trade Marks in the UK. It was introduced in 2009 and is aimed at helping people and businesses register Trade Marks more easily and cheaply in the UK without using a lawyer or Trade Mark attorney. Unlike previous systems, the Right Start Service enables you to defer 50% of the application fee until after the application has been assessed by the Trade Mark examiner who determines whether the mark can be registered.

Under the Right Start Service, if there are any problems with the Trade Mark application, the applicant can discuss them with the Trade Mark examiner, make some changes to ensure it meets the requirements, and then continue with the application and pay the remaining fees. The objective is to increase the success in registering Trade Marks, whilst helping people to do it more cost-effectively; a real win-win for businesses.

All Trade Mark applications are assessed by an examiner, who checks if the mark and the application meet the legal requirements for a Trade Mark. When I applied for my first Trade Mark myself under this service, I made errors in completing the documentation; in fact I got lots of things wrong as I was not fully aware of what I needed to do.
I received the examiners report, which explained the parts of my application which did not meet the requirements; the most useful part of the report gave recommendations for amendment to ensure the application met the legal requirements. This meant I could edit my application, pay the balance of the fees and the application was accepted for publication.

As I have registered many Trade Marks using the Right Start Service, I have learnt from my mistakes, but there are sometimes 'queries' listed on the examination report that are unforeseen. Personally, I have always tried to telephone the examiner to discuss the report and what I need to do to overcome any objections, so I have the highest probability of acceptance and registration. There is a 'Standard Service' for registering a Trade Mark, but it does not allow you to make changes to the original application; this is why the Right Start Service is invaluable, practical and successful.

CAN I REGISTER MY OWN TRADE MARKS IN OTHER COUNTRIES?

It is possible to register your Trade Mark in many countries around the world. The more countries you register in, the wider your protection. But Trade Marks are regional or territorial; if you apply for a UK Trade Mark your rights extend to the UK only, similarly a Trade Mark in the USA gives protection in the USA only. Generally you apply for a Trade Mark for each individual country you wish to register in, with the exception of the European Union where there is a Harmonized System enabling one application to cover all EU member states.

On a global basis, it is possible to apply for an International Trade Mark, which covers more than 70 countries throughout the world, including the UK, USA, EU and Australia. Application is made through the World Intellectual Property Orgaisation (WIPO), and you can select all countries or just some of the countries listed. Requirements and costs vary, and even though it may seem prudent to register in as many countries as possible, it may not be practical or commercially viable. Also, due to the variance in systems and requirements around the world, it us usually necessary to have a professional Trade Mark lawyer undertake a multi-country registration on your behalf.

REGISTERING A TRADE MARK THROUGHOUT THE EU

If you are selling your products or services to a country within the European Union, you can apply for a Community Trade Mark (CTM) through the Community Trade Mark Office (formerly the Office for Harmonization in the Internal Market, known as OHIM). The Community Trade Mark gives protection in all EU member states, but to be successful the application must be acceptable to ALL member states; therefore if the application fails in one state, the whole application is rejected. If you are planning to trade within Europe, it is wise to apply for a CTM, but as this application covers all member states, opposition can be raised from anyone within the EU (including the UK).

The UK's Right Start Service shares many similarities with the system in place in the EU for registering a Community Trade Mark (CTM). The online applications systems are similarly structured. In understanding how to register UK Trade Marks, I have been able to also register my own CTM's, again without using a lawyer and saving myself considerable sums of money. The main difference with the CTM process is the official fees are higher and are paid in full at application. However I have always been able to discuss with the examiner of the CTM if I needed to, and make changes to the application before it is published, to maximise the chance of registration.

My experience of registering a UK Trade Mark made all the difference when I first applied for a CTM; I understood the process, the information required and also how to research my mark before applying. I would recommend using the UK Right Start Service to register a simple Trade Mark before embarking on a full CTM registration yourself as the experience is invaluable to get it right first time.

I'M NOT IN THE UK OR EU, CAN I STILL APPLY TO REGISTER MY OWN TRADE MARK IN THESE AREAS?

The UK's Intellectual Property Office can only correspond with applicants who are located in the UK, the European Economic Area (EEA) or the Channel Isles.

It is possible to register your own Trade Mark (UK or EU) if you live outside these regions providing you have a correspondent address within the region. For example, you or your business could be located in Australia, and if you used a representative, an agent or even a local employee as your contact address, you can still hold your own Trade Mark registration.
In this case, when applying for a Trade Mark, the name of the person applying for the mark would be a Representative or Agent of the applicant.

WHAT IS A TRADE MARK AND WHAT PROTECTION DOES IT GIVE ME?

According to the Intellectual Property Office, a Trade Mark is a "symbol that distinguishes goods and services in the marketplace" including brand names, words and logos, from your competitors.

A registered Trade Mark shows your customers you are the originator of your product or service, it can add extra value to your company as it can be an asset of the business, and it can also increase the professionalism and positioning in your market, especially against competitors.

Holding the registered Trade Mark for what you do differentiates you from your competitors; it can increase recognition with your clients and customers whilst protecting your brand, name or company from being copied.

As the owner of a registered Trade Mark, you have powerful protection of your mark, with the legal right to:

- Stop anyone else from commercially using an identical mark for identical products or services;
- Stop someone else using a similar Trade Mark for similar products or services which could confuse potential or existing customers;
- Stop third parties from using your registered Trade Mark on any products, services, business papers, advertising, packaging;
- Stop the import or export of products using your registered Trade Mark.

If any of your Trade Mark rights are infringed, the courts have the authority to stop these infringements.

As well as stopping someone from using your registered Trade Mark, you also have the right to allow someone to use the registered Trade Mark. For instance, you could agree to license your Trade Mark to another person or company, who in turn would pay you a fee for using it.
Should you get to a stage where you no longer wish to own the Trade Mark, you can 'sell' or assign the Trade Mark to a new owner, which again generates revenue.

If you have invested considerable time, money and effort in building your company name, brand or logo to be recognised by your customers, it is important you protect this. It is your Intellectual Property - it is what you can do, what you know and more importantly it allows you to be recognised as the creator or founder of these properties.

If you do not protect your Intellectual Property, enabling you to enforce your rights and protect your business, you can lose sales, reputation and position with your customers. Without protection you have very little recourse, and if someone infringes your Trade Mark and is not stopped, others will usually do the same very quickly.

WHAT IS THE DIFFERENCE BETWEEN A TRADE MARK AND COPYRIGHT?

Trade Mark and Copyright are two completely separate areas of Intellectual Property. There can be some crossover, especially in terms of images or unique logos, but whilst copyright can protect artwork, Trade Mark can protect the name and brand.

COPYRIGHT

Copyright is automatically granted if you, your business or your employees create an original 'Work'. This protection is something you have, not something you do, and is in force as as soon the Work is recorded in some way (e.g. written, stored etc), regardless of the medium in which the Work exists, including the internet.

A copyrighted Work cannot be made, copied, rented, loaned or issued without your permission. This means you can take action to stop any infringement to your copyright, but it is what is called a 'private right', meaning it is your responsibility to take action if anyone infringes your copyright by using part or whole of the Work without your permission.

Copyright gives you the exclusive right to produce copies and control the original Work. It covers:

- Literary works: novels, books, computer programmes, web pages, instruction manuals, song lyrics, articles and layout or arrangement used to publish a work;
- Music to songs, sound recordings, videos, films and dramatic works including dance and mime;
- Art, drawings (both artistic and technical), photographs, engravings, sculptures, architecture, images, diagrams, collages and maps;
- Electronic and paper-based databases;
- Broadcast.

You can't copyright an idea.

Copyright does not protect names, hook-lines, phrases or slogans, nor does it cover products, services or processes.

Copyright is automatic; in the UK, and throughout the EU, you do not have to register a copyright.

Copyright is independent of the medium in which the Work was first created. For example, if you hold the copyright to a Work in a particular medium e.g. print, and someone copies it in another medium e.g. web, you are protected. Similarly, if you have written a book and someone makes an audio recording of it, this infringes your copyright too.

Remember: if you use a third party (e.g. a designer) to create something for you such as a logo, a website or a video recording, they retain copyright unless it is specifically assigned to you in a contract. You must ensure you own copyright for your properties because if you do not, you are licensing the work from the originator for your use; they retain copyright and they can stop you from using it in the future.

To identify a Work, including your web pages, as your copyright, the copyright symbol '©' must be displayed along with the name or the copyright holder (person, company or organisation) and the date.

Traditionally the term 'All Rights Reserved' was used to declare that the copyright holder was retaining all the rights. Convention now states this is not necessary as international copyright agreements already confer all rights; however many authors (self included) prefer to include this statement even though it is no longer necessary.

TRADE MARKS

A Trade Mark indicates the ownership, quality, and/or origin of goods or services, which associates those goods or services with an individual or a company.

Trade Marks are usually logos, words or a combination of both, but they can also be names, initials, letters, symbols, sign, sounds or music (such as jingles). These are sometimes referred to as a device.
If the device is a word or a series of words but created in a certain design layout, this can be known as being 'stylised', an Image Mark or Figurative Mark.
A 'stylised' word, phrase or slogan does not refer to or cover a particular font in which it is written - it refers to the layout and the design as a whole.

You can Trade Mark a phrase, slogan, brand name, your company name, a form of packaging or even a gesture.

One of the few gestures which is Trade Marked in the UK is registered by Asda Supermarkets: on their television advertisements - the tap on the back pocket (also known as 'the buttock slap') is a Trade Mark !

Nearly all Trade Marks are made of words, images or a combination of both. These 'ordinary' marks are also known as word marks or image marks. If a combination of words in a stylised format or the words form part of the logo, these can be known as figurative marks, image marks or combination marks; the terms are interchangeable.

DESIGNING THE BRAND

When I am working on a new brand, image or logo, I research beforehand to check I am not infringing anyone else's Trade Mark or Copyright. I will then talk with my designer about a logo, name and/or hook line.

I want the name and logo to always be distinctive, which helps customer recognition and aids the Trade Mark registration.
One of the best ways to create a distinctive name is to make up a word or use two or more conjoined words. A great example comes from a friend of mine who runs a company that supplies information to pharmacists. He has taken the two key words and named his company The Informacist, from INFORMation and pharmACIST. It is a completely original name from two words conjoined and is therefore distinctive.

Alternatively the name may not relate to the product or service, it can just be a name or word which does not associate with the goods or service, but with the brand; the more original the better. Well known examples are Amazon and Kindle - both words are known, both unrelated to what they sell, but are a distinctive name for the brand.

A Word mark can give wider and stronger protection than an image mark (logo with words). An image mark only gives you rights for the combination of the words and the logo together, not the separate elements, but a Word mark means no one else can use those words, either as a word mark or as part of an image mark.

A hook or tag line is usually descriptive and explains the benefits delivered. It is focused on the problem solved: how the customer's life is made easier, saves them money, time and/or resources.

If I intend to use a logo or stylise the name to launch a product or service, I always ask the designer to create three versions of the mark: one with the ™ symbol next to it, one with the ® symbol next to it, and one without either symbol.
As soon as I launch and apply for the Mark to be registered, I publicly use the ™ version to show this is our property, but it is an unregistered Trade Mark.
I use the version without either symbol to submit as part of my Trade Mark application; an application for an type of mark cannot be submitted with either of these symbols next to them.
Once the Trade Mark is registered, I can simply update the mark and use the version with the ® symbol to show that it is a registered Trade Mark.

DO I HAVE TO WORRY ABOUT THE FONT AND COLOURS OF A TRADE MARK?

When you apply to register a Trade Mark, the Mark is recorded exactly as it is in the application form and your registered rights are for the mark as filed.

Where a Trade Mark is registered with a specific colour combination, your registered rights are for the mark in those colours.

When registering a Word mark, you do not need to specify the font type used and if a similar mark (depending on the similarity of the font according to the examiner) is filed for similar products or services you should still have infringement rights.

There are no specific rules and each case is assessed individually by the examiner with regard to the impact any different colours or fonts have on the mark, and the classification of the products or services the mark is used on.

ARE ALL MARKS ALLOWED?

Trade Marks must be distinctive, meaning they distinguish your products, goods or services from your competitors and other companies offering similar goods and services.
The most important thing to remember is a Trade Mark must not try to describe what is being sold, the mark must be distinctive.

It must not mislead people about the nature of your products or services, or mislead customers perception of the features, benefits or qualities of the products or services.

A Trade Mark cannot be registered if it is offensive, is against the law or is a 'specially protected emblem' such as The Olympic Symbol, National flags of countries, The Royal Crown or Emblems of a Country.

Likewise, a Trade Mark that describes the products or services or shows the quality, quantity, purpose, value or geographic origin cannot be registered.

If a word or mark has become an established or accepted mark within your business sector, this cannot be registered either. For example, the word Escalator was originally a Trade Mark. As the popularity of the 'moving staircase' increased, it became known by its brand name, and eventually lost its distinctiveness and became descriptive; the Trade Mark was then revoked even though it was registered.
This does not happen very frequently, but it can.

WHAT IS DISTINCTIVE VERSUS DESCRIPTIVE?

For a Trade Mark application to be accepted and subsequently registered, it must be distinctive, not descriptive. This is one area most people misunderstand when they first start out.

Distinctive means it has uniqueness, it can be associated with what you do and is distinguishable from others. Descriptive means the mark actually tells you what it does

For example, the domain name for this ebook website is
TradeMarksMadeEasy.com.
Even though this is the only domain name of its kind, and is therefore unique, it is descriptive. If it was not a domain name, but separate words, it would read Trade Marks Made Easy. The name gives an exact representation of what the product is, and what it does; it is descriptive and therefore can't be registered as a Trade Mark.

There are many titles of books, websites and TV programmes that include 'Made Easy', such as Gardening Made Easy, Chinese Food Made Easy and Drawing Made Easy. There are also websites with similar names e.g. Patents Made Easy, and again this title cannot be Trade Marked as it is in general and accepted use (and is descriptive).

To make it distinctive, I could add my company name to the title, to become 'GJ International Trade Marks Made Easy'. This would associate the mark with my company, not confuse customers and could give the required level of distinctiveness as the product can be from my company only.

One way to be distinctive is to create new words, conjoin words or misspell words, but the new word or misspelling must be noticeable.
Using this ebook's title as an example again, it could be TradeMarksMadEasy, where there is only one E between Made and Easy: trademarksmadEasy.
Interestingly when I approached the IPO and discussed this with them, even though it is a deliberate spelling mistake, the examiner believed that by omitting one of the E's the title does not read differently to the version with the correct spelling, so therefore it may be confusing and not have the required level of distinction.
If you go for using a spelling mistake, ensure it obvious and noticeable.

Another option, and the one I used for the Community Trade Mark for this book title, is to create distinctiveness in a visual way by creating a logo which includes the title or name. The Trade Marks Made Easy logo of this book is Trade Marked throughout Europe, but it is the image that is protected, not the individual words.

If you decide to create distinctiveness for something that is descriptive by using a logo or an image to create a device, the image or logo cannot reinforce the words. For instance, if you were trying to Trade Mark the word 'House' for a building project; firstly you could not simply Trade Mark the word as it is descriptive of its application, not distinctive. If you tried to make it distinctive by adding a logo of a house, then even if the entire logo and word together were unique, the logo would further reinforce the word and actually increase the descriptiveness, not the distinctiveness. You can create a stylised version of the word by using a text design to give distinctiveness, but it cannot reinforce the mark.

A business associate of mine has a registered Trade Mark for the word 'GOLD' within the class for financial services. The word GOLD is heavily stylised to make it a logo as opposed to being pure text. In this way the logo can be visually associated with his company and is therefore distinctive.

The word GOLD is a registered Trade Mark (but not stylised) by other companies, none of whom are in financial services and therefore it could be argued the word GOLD is distinctive and not descriptive, being a name for their product or service and not associated with their industry or precious metals (for example).

In financial services, using the word GOLD could be seen as reinforcing the brand and also be misleading to potential customers, as GOLD could be viewed as a currency or financial outcome. Using a stylised mark however makes it distinctive and something customers can associate with, but protection is only for the mark as it is registered and therefore only the stylised GOLD image mark carries protection, not the word.

Very often distinctiveness can be more effective for an element or part of a product or service. I was copied by a competitor a few years ago. I was running a business development workshop call Marketing for SMEs, and this competitor started to run a similar event, with almost identical content and title to mine.

I had built up a high reputation in the local business community for this workshop; the other company wanted to jump on my bandwagon and try to take my success. The name of the workshop, Marketing for SMEs, is completely descriptive and therefore cannot be registered; I could not stop them from using the same title.

Part of the content of my workshop I called the Rules of Don't®, which is a unique made up phrase I use, with the comment that the opposite of what you should do isn't always what you shouldn't do, and therefore these Rules of Don't® are what you shouldn't do.

The rules all start with 'Don't...' and then an explanatory sentence of what you shouldn't do.

As the Rules of Don't® are unique and distinctive, I decided to register it as Word Mark and use it in the promotion of the workshops. The Trade Mark is registered and is protected in three different classes.

Class 16: Printed Publications

Class 35: Business consultancy services

Class 41:Training workshops services

I now use the Rules of Don't® in all my content (workshops, books, consulting etc). As I own the registered Trade Mark, anyone trying to copy me is infringing my Trade Mark and I have full legal protection.

I use Rules of Don't® in proactive marketing: instead of concentrating on the DESCRIPTIVE title of a workshop or a book, I now focus on the DISTINCTIVE elements within it, so clients and customers can associate what I deliver with the unique name, and to ensure there is no confusion with competitors who may try to encroach on my business.

WHAT IS A REGISTERED TRADE MARK AND AN UNREGISTERED TRADE MARK AND WHAT PROTECTION DO THEY GIVE ME?

There are two ways to show you are using the device as a Trade Mark.

REGISTERED TRADE MARKS

A registered Trade Mark carries the validity and automatic protection rights that are granted once registered. You can place the ® symbol against your mark. Note: it is illegal to use the ® symbol if the mark is not an officially registered Trade Mark.

If your registered Trade Mark, or a similar one, is used by anyone else for the products or service for which you hold the registered Trade Mark, you have the automatic right to sue for infringement.

A restraining order can be applied to stop the infringement. Damages and costs can be awarded. Also, if your Trade Mark is infringed due to import of counterfeit products, you can stop these imports if you suspect your rights have been abused.

Pursuing an infringement requires legal action, which can result in court hearings and the need to work with a legally qualified representative.

UNREGISTERED TRADE MARKS

Using the ™ symbol shows your Trade Mark is unregistered but you are aware of your Trade Mark rights. It says to competitors and customers you are serious and you are using that particular logo or name as a Trade Mark in your business. You should do this immediately for all logos or names which are important to your business. It is free to do but the mark is unregistered and therefore you have no legal protection.

Even though you may have been using your Mark with the letters ™ against it, someone else can still apply to register your mark. The fact that you have placed ™ after your mark will not affect the examination process of the application, or the outcome of the examination, but you may oppose the application once it is published in the Trade Mark Journal. Just because you have used the ™ symbol, it does not give you sole right to oppose an application for registration; anyone can oppose an application.

If you decide to apply to register your Mark, having used the letters ™ does not provide evidence of distinctiveness. If you apply for registration and are relying on 'acquired distinctiveness', the examiner will look at all factors when considering the evidence including the use of the Device as a Trade Mark, the customer recognition and the period of time in use. You must demonstrate use, and relate and prove the distinctiveness you have acquired through its use.

If you decide not to register your Mark, you could be placing your Mark, your intellectual property and your business in a very vulnerable position.

WHAT IS TRADE MARK INFRINGEMENT?

If you have a registered Trade Mark and someone else uses an identical or similar Trade Mark for identical or similar products or service, this may be a case of Trade Mark infringement, especially if the use of the mark could cause confusion in the eyes of your customers.

Infringement can also occur where non-identical Trade Marks cause confusion with customers who incorrectly believe the products or services are from the same supplier.

If a registered Trade Mark has a high reputation in the marketplace, and another same or similar mark, that doesn't cause confusion with customers (i.e. different products or services) but takes advantage of that reputation or even damages the reputation of the Trade Mark, this may be classed as infringement too.

If you believe a mark, whether registered or unregistered is infringing your Trade Mark, you must seek legal advice from a Trade Mark professional. Successfully defending a Trade Mark largely depends on getting it right in the first place.

Conversely, if you are considering offering products or services under a Trade Mark, you must make sure you will not be infringing anyone else's mark before you first use it, whether registered or not. If the mark is already registered, or one similar to it, you could be sued for infringement even if your infringement was unintentional. Penalties for Trade Mark infringement can include a restraining order, fines including costs and damages and even charges of counterfeiting which carry a custodial sentence.

If the mark is unregistered, then Passing Off would need to be proved which is time consuming, costly and extremely difficult to evidence damages incurred. If successful, an injunction could be put in place and costs and damages awarded.

You are responsible for enforcing the rights of your Trade Mark. If you think there is a case of infringement, it is up to you to decide what action you wish to take. Personally I would gather factual, dated evidence and discuss with a Trade Mark professional.

WHAT IS PASSING OFF?

Passing Off is misrepresentations made by one business that can damage the reputation or goodwill of another business, such as trying to Pass Off products or services as those of another company.

If someone adopts the same or similar Mark as your own unregistered Trade Mark, to present their products or services as yours without your permission, you can take action against them but you have to rely on the common law of tort of 'Passing Off' to protect your rights. This is both time consuming and extremely expensive as all cases require evidence and there is no guarantee of success.

To be successful in a Passing Off action, you or your company must provide factual evidence that:

- The mark is yours, you have built up a reputation in the mark and goodwill from your customer's perspective;
- Your business has lost, or is likely to lose, business or revenue as a result of the use of the offending Trade Mark; and
- The offending mark could cause, or has caused, confusion with your mark.

There is no legal definition of these three elements and the most difficult to prove is goodwill as it is subjective and varies by customer.

Remember you must provide <u>factual evidence</u> of the harm (loss or likely loss of business or revenue) which has been, or will be, caused through the offending mark. This is why it can be very difficult, expensive and time consuming to prove a Passing Off action.

If (and it is a big IF) you are successful in your Passing Off action, an injunction can be served on the offender and you can also be awarded damages and costs - but this again relies on the factual evidence.

Registering your Trade Mark means it is easier and more straightforward to take legal action against infringement of your mark as you have automatic rights for your registered Trade Mark. Passing Off is far from clear-cut and can be subjective with no guarantee of outcomes.

I HAVE A UK LIMITED COMPANY AND I OWN THE DOMAIN NAME, THIS MEANS I OWN THE TRADE MARK…DOESN'T IT?

Many people believe they are protected if they have registered their company name as a UK limited company (or EU country equivalent), and they own their domain name (web address) of their company or product/ services. This is TOTALLY WRONG!
In UK law, the registered company name, the Trade Mark and the Domain Name are all completely separate.

Regardless of how long you have owned the domain name or company, these do not provide any registered Trade Mark protection. The only way to have the protection is to register your Trade Mark.

WHAT IS TRADE MARK SQUATTING?

The best way to explain Trade Mark Squatting is to give a scenario:
I could research your company name, logo, domain name and the goods or services you offer, and if you do not have a registered Trade Mark, I could apply to register your mark as my Trade Mark. Providing there is no current registered Trade Mark for your brand, company or name applied to these goods or services, I could then own the registered Trade Mark for your brand. As I then have the registered rights over that mark I can send you a Cease and Desist instruction and if you continue trading, I could sue you for infringing my registered Trade Mark; I could stop you trading under your current company name, domain name or using your brand. I could even offer to license or sell your original mark back to you.

This may seem unrealistic or improbable, but there are many cases where this has happened including family members, business partners or unrelated third-parties registering the mark and holding the rights over it. This is known as 'squatting'; registering the Trade Mark with the intention of selling it back to the owner for a profit, or trying to take control of the Mark.

If this did occur and you happened to find out that I was registering your mark, you could oppose the registration on grounds of Passing Off. You would be obliged to provide factual evidence of how it would detrimentally affect the goodwill you have created in your brand or company with your customers. As stated previously, Passing Off is complicated, time consuming and an expensive process with no guarantee of success.

The best way to protect yourself against Squatting is to register your logo, hook line, company name, your domain name, your own name or initials, images, or any combination of these as a registered Trade Mark which will give you full legal protection against any form of infringement or Squatting.

CAN I REGISTER MY WEBSITE DOMAIN AS A TRADEMARK?

A domain name is the name an individual, company, brand, product or service is known by on the internet. Owning a domain name does not give any registered Trade Mark protection regardless of how many years you may have owned the domain name, whether the domain name is in use or not, or the number of visitors you get to your site.

If you have a registered Trade Mark and own the domain name, it can be good business practice and give further protection to Trade Mark the domain name(s) too. A Trade Marked domain name can give more traction as far as search engine optimisation is concerned, and can potentially strengthen your brand.

Many lawyers recommend this because a registered domain name as a Trade Mark not only gives you the right to use the mark on your products or services, but also over the internet. Therefore if you experience a conflict with a domain name you will be in a very strong position to defend your brand.

When registering a domain name, the www. part of the domain name is not usually stated in the application as it is generic. The registration would include the Top Level Domain (TLD) suffix i.e. the .com, .co.uk, .net .eu, which identifies the mark as a domain name.

The TLD forms part of the entire Trade Mark to identify it as a domain name, but as the TLD is generic, you do not have full protected rights over this suffix; you do have protection for the entire domain name as a mark.

Your ownership and use of your domain name does not automatically mean you will be granted a registered Trade Mark for it. Your domain name may not satisfy the requirements for registration as there may be Trade Marks (non-domain name or domain names) already registered which could be similar to your domain name, your domain could be similar to someone else's Trade Mark and therefore cause confusion, or it could be descriptive or indistinctive and not meet the requirements in this way.

Similarly, if you have a registered Trade Mark, this does not entitle you to use that mark as a domain name. As mentioned previously, the same Trade Mark can be registered for different products or services (depending on the classes in which it is registered) by different companies or individuals. The domain name may be in legitimate use for another product or service, or be in use for unregistered products or services.

If you believe someone is using your domain name for Passing Off their products or services as yours, or they are Squatters and have registered the Trade Mark of your domain name just to sell it back to you, then you may be able to take legal action.

WHAT ARE SERIES MARKS?

Series marks are a number of Trade Marks, up to a maximum of six marks, which are substantially the same, resembling each other. The detail of each of the marks is basically the same, the only difference being 'non distinctive characters' which have no effect on the identity of the mark. This means each mark in the series has a small difference and therefore they are not identical.

A series mark is important where there are a number of ways of representing your mark. For example, if you register a word as your mark in all capitals, and then use it written in italics, the italicised version is not the way it was registered and therefore is not a registered Trade Mark.

For example, if I were to apply to register my company name (omitting the Ltd suffix):

GJ International

The series could be:

GJ International (italicised)
G.J. International (with full stops after the initials)
GJ INTERNATIONAL (in all capitals)
GJInternational (conjoined)

In this example, each of the series marks differs from the mark applied for, but all are basically the same, whether combined or in upper or lower case. If a customer were to read each of the series, they would identify with the original mark applied for because the words 'separate naturally'. This is a simplified example to show the way a series mark works (as the registration is for the words, not the font).

Series marks are usually applied to figurative marks where the logo or image is used or displayed in different colours on the product or service, with each colour variant being one of the series.

Series marks can be quite complicated as each change in the series is examined separately to ensure it resembles every other mark in the series. It is possible for an examiner to accept or reject some of the series marks applied for but not all. The main consideration is that any differences are non-distinctive and do not affect the identities of the marks.

As the majority of marks are visual, any mark in the series should not have a substantial effect on the visual conceptual identity of the series of marks or the distinctiveness. For example, you can Trade Mark a signature, and you can Trade Mark the same name but in type face; however as the different styles would affect the conceptual identity and distinctiveness of the marks, they cannot be a series; the signature and the name in type face would require completely separate applications as even though they say the same thing (the name), and may be used for exactly the same goods or services, they look completely different.

Another consideration is where the meaning can change or be misconstrued. The example given by a Trade Mark examiner was of a case rejected for a series mark. The Mark applied for was: Peoples Team, with a series application for both words conjoined.

When both words were conjoined they formed: peoplesteam

which can be misinterpreted as: People Steam, and not Peoples Team.

The two words together may not be perceived as the words applied for in the mark, therefore an objection was raised by the examiner. This may seem pedantic, but it does change the conceptual identity if misread.

An application for a series mark can be made in the UK under the Right Start Service, but there is no option for a series mark when applying for a Community Trade Mark.

SERIES MARKS AND DOMAIN NAMES

It is possible to Trade Mark domain names as a series. For example, the directory site The Ant Can could register the domain names:
    theantcan.com
    theantcan.co.uk

As the .co.uk and the .com suffixes are understood to be domain names and easily recognised, they do not substantially affect the identities of the mark and therefore constitute a series mark

However, the following would not be acceptable:
    The Ant Can
    theantcan.com
    theantcan.co.uk

The first mark is not automatically recognisable as a domain name and therefore the conceptual identity is different from the other marks in the series.

If you wish to apply for a series of marks, undertake your research and ask the IPO for advice. They cannot give any decisions as this is for the examiner when the series mark is applied for, but they can give advice and direct you to other sources of information.

ARE SERIES MARKS REALLY NECESSARY?

If I am registering a unique image mark, it should have its own level of distinctiveness. If I register it in one form, but not as a series (in different colours for example), I only have full protection for the mark as represented in the registration. However if someone else tries to register a mark similar or identical to my unique mark for the same, or similar goods or service, the examiner should uncover the similarity during the examination process and I will be advised. I can then potentially oppose the other party's application, perhaps on the grounds that it is confusingly similar.

With a Word mark you have protection for the words, not the font. Therefore a change in font may not be necessary to enhance the protection further. Also, if another person tries to register a figurative mark, which includes an image/logo and the words as per your registration, this could constitute an infringement.

The majority of applications for image marks are made with the mark being in greyscale; word marks are usually in block capitals. Some say this is just convention, however it does show the mark more generally, not in a specific colour set or font type. If the mark is shown in a particular colour, it is only protected for that colour; if in greyscale, it may be harder for a similar application to prove it is not confusingly similar if in a specific colour.

Tip: before applying for a series mark, decide whether it is really necessary as your mark may have sufficient distinctiveness and originality, and any other application by another party could be confusingly similar, which could mean a series mark is not necessary.

You do not have to use your mark exactly as you have registered it, providing any differences do not change its distinctiveness. For example, you may register a word mark using a particular font, but you will still have protection for your mark if it is written in another font as long as it is the word(s) that are distinctive, not the font. If however you register an image mark in a particular colour, and that colour is associated with the mark, then changing the colour could mean the mark loses its distinctiveness and therefore would need to be included as a series.

CAN I TRADE MARK MY INITIALS?

A registration for two or more letters (your initials for example) would normally be accepted unless there is a specific reason why the combination would not be accepted as a Trade Mark, such as they are an acronym which is already generally well known.

If accepted, the Trade Mark is only applicable to the combination they are filed in; changing the order, duplicating the initials or even separating them with full stops would cause the mark to be visually different and therefore seen as separate marks. In this case a separate application to register each combination would be required.

Can I Trade Mark my name?

A simple answer is Yes, as long as no one has already registered the same name in the same classes.

A Trade Mark does not have to be a word for an object, it can be your name. This is especially useful as many business consultants use their name for their company, and their recognition and authenticity is based on it.

WHAT ARE TRADE MARK CLASSES?

When you register a Trade Mark you must specify the scope of protection for your goods or services by their Primary Use. This is done by selecting the relevant 'class' and adding a description that relates to the primary use. There are 45 different classes; 34 covering products and 11 covering services. You can register in one class, or a number of classes for the same Trade Mark.

An overview of the various classes, with brief descriptions of relating products or service, is in the appendix at the end of this book. This is not a complete list and an accurate search must be undertaken during your research before applying for your mark.

A registered Trade Mark is only protected under the classes specified at the time of registration. This means two identical Trade Marks can exist in different classes and be registered by different companies/individuals.

When selecting the class or classes for your Trade Mark, you should select the one(s) based on the primary use(s) of your goods or service. Sometimes this can be obvious, for example if I am going to use my company logo as a Trade Mark covering the delivery of business consultancy and training workshops, I would opt for Class 35 (Business Consultancy) and Class 41 (Provision of Training).

Even though my logo would be printed on my letterhead and displayed on my website, I would not necessarily register under Class 16 (Printed Matter) as this is not the primary use of the product or service.

This ebook and its website is all about Trade Marks; if I were giving legal advice this would be registered under Class 45 (Advice on Trade Marks), but as this is a Downloadable Electronic Publication, it is Class 09. The website however is not 'primary use'; it is the marketing mechanism. People purchase the book, not the website services. The usage does not cover the subject matter, it is the primary use of the product or service.

It is highly important to get the classes right first time as once the Trade Mark is registered these cannot be extended without applying for a completely new Trade Mark registration.

Identical Trade Marks can be registered by separate companies or individuals in different classes.
For example, the word LAKELAND is registered by separate companies for different products such as Chemical Protective Clothing (Class 09), Pencils (Class 16) and Cooking Apparatus (Class 11) and it is listed under many other classes. This co-existence relates to the class and the products or services specified within the class.

LAKELAND is listed by separate companies under the same class; the difference being the description or item within that class.

One registrant has listed the products as 'Pencils' in Class 16, whereas another registrant has listed a whole range of other products under Class 16 as: "Paper goods for household purposes; paper goods for hygiene and sanitary purposes; stationery; tablecloths and napkins; plastic wrapping; printed matter; document wallets of card and/or plastic; albums; plastic storage bags; wrapping materials; but not including writing materials or goods of a similar nature to these excluded goods."
The last sentence "but not including writing materials or goods of a similar nature to these excluded goods" means that they have not claimed any

rights for Pencils, and therefore do not infringe the other Trade Mark registration.

LAKELAND STONE is registered in Class 02, but if this were to be registered in other classes where LAKELAND is already registered, and both had similar descriptions, it may be considered too similar to LAKELAND as the word STONE may not be sufficiently distinctive and cause confusion with customers.

Notice the descriptions state the primary use of the products or services, it is not a list of the background, the benefits or an explanation of the product or service.

Tip: When I am researching for a new Trade Mark application, I always review the classes and descriptions of similar marks, or those used in similar industries. I make notes of the classes and the various sentences used in the descriptions, and use these as a reference that I can adapt when making my own application.

The descriptions of goods or services can overlap across classes. When the examiner reviews your application, any registered marks that are similar or identical within the stated classes will be identified, but in addition a cross-search will be made to check for similar or identical marks in related classes; the examination report may include a classification query or/and list earlier marks identified which are the same, or similar, to the goods or services listed in your application but in different classes.

The class or classes of the device you intend to Trade Mark must be researched accurately. The easiest way to find the classes is to use the IPO site's search facility. I repeat the search with as many variations of the Search Words as possible to check for all possible classes.

The same search words can show up in a number of different classes, as there may be cross-overs between the use of goods and services. I make notes of each of the classes and their descriptors that relate to the primary use of my goods or services. I also search for singular and plural versions of words, as these may fall into different descriptions too.

Classes and descriptions can be searched during the application under the Right Start service, where the site automatically lists the accepted descriptions by class. Personally I prefer to have information before I start the application to ensure I do not miss any details.

WHAT IS THE NICE CLASSIFICATION?

The Nice Classification is an international, multilateral agreement that is recognised in numerous countries, and throughout the EU. It establishes standard classes and descriptions of goods and services for the purpose of registering Trade Marks.

The first agreement was made in Nice, France in 1957, and hence carries the name of where it was signed. All EU Community Trade Marks (CTM's) use the Nice Classification system, which also relates to the UK classification system too.

The benefits of the Nice Classification is it's standardised approach; it is very simple to use and understand, with the descriptions of the goods and services being selectable from a pre-defined list within each class. Each descriptor has been accepted by all countries that have signed up to this agreement; this means you do not have to decide the wording that you should use for the description, you simply select it from the list and know it is the correct wording. Obviously you have to select the correct classes, but the standardisation makes it a lot easier.

A further advantage is when searching international Trade Marks. If they are registered using the Nice Classification, there will be a translation into other languages.

When you apply for your UK Trade Mark or Community Trade Mark, you will use a search and select system during the application process which includes the standardised Nice Classification descriptions of the goods and services by class.

WHAT ARE CERTIFICATE AND COLLECTIVE MARKS?

The majority of Trade Mark applications are for 'ordinary' marks (logos, names, images etc), which identify the mark owners' goods or services.

There are also two other types of mark: Certificate Mark or Collective Mark. These marks are very rarely registered, but when applying for your mark online you will be asked whether your mark is a Certificate Mark or a Collective Mark. The probability is your mark will not be either of these (as you will be registering an ordinary mark) and therefore you will leave these fields blank on the application. However, it is important to understand what each of these types of marks are.

CERTIFICATE MARK

A Certificate Mark is usually registered in the name of a professional or technical body, standards institute, trade association or government department. A Certificate Mark is intended to differentiate between goods and services that meet a defined standard or attribute from those that do not. It shows the goods or services have been tested, inspected or examined against specific criteria by an independent organisation.

COLLECTIVE MARK

A Collective Mark is usually owned by a trade association, and identifies that the goods or services are provided by a member of the association; the Collective Mark gives differentiation to those who are entitled to use it. The association owns the registered Trade Mark for the benefit of its members; the Collective Mark does not identify the particular goods or services supplied, only the membership of the association and the entitlement to display the mark.

Certification and Collective Marks are complicated but rarely used.

WHAT IS PRIORITY, EXHIBITION PRIORITY AND SENIORITY?

PRIORITY CLAIMS

During the application, you can claim Priority for your Trade Mark if you have applied for this mark outside the UK (or EU for a Community Trade Mark application) within the last 6 months; if you haven't, just skip it.

Where you have made an application in another country and are claiming Priority, you will need to include the relevant details, classes and evidence of it when you make your new application. At least one of the classes of the previous application must be the same as for this new application, and the country in which you made the original application must have signed up to the Paris Convention for the Protection of Industrial Property. This can be checked by searching Google and the World Intellectual Property Organization.

EXHIBITION PRIORITY

When applying for a Community Trade Mark you can claim Exhibition Priority.
Exhibition Priority relates to the date when you displayed your goods or services for the first time in the public domain. It can only be claimed if the

first public display was at an officially recognised exhibition, and you must support this claim with documentary evidence when you apply for your CTM. Exhibition Priority is not open-ended; you have 6 months from the first public display to make this claim. If you apply for a CTM and the first public disclosure was more than 6 months prior, you cannot claim Exhibition Priority and should therefore leave this blank on the CTM application.

SENIORITY

The EU Community Trade Mark allows claims to Seniority. Do not confuse Seniority with Priority; they are different. Seniority is where you consolidate marks and literally merge a Community Trade Mark with an earlier identical Trade Mark registered in another EU state. The mark must be identical in every way including the owner, classes and descriptions. If you are new to Trade Marks, you will probably not be claiming Seniority.

WHAT ARE LIMITATIONS AND DISCLAIMERS?

If you wish to (or need to) voluntarily limit the rights of your Trade Mark, or disclaim the exclusive use of a specified element of your mark, you will need to add details when making your application.
You may wish to limit the territory you are covered in or limit particular goods or services within a class.

Where part of your mark is used elsewhere and therefore you cannot state it is unique or distinctive, you can disclaim exclusivity to part of your mark.
If your mark is a play on generic words, then you may want to consider a limitation or disclaimer as you will be renouncing your rights for that particular part or element of the mark.

In reality, and as with the nearly every application, your mark is probably unique; therefore you will not need to disclaim or limit anything. You leave this section blank on the application. If you are unsure, you should discuss with the examiner.

HOW ARE TRADE MARK APPLICATIONS ASSESSED?

This single question is probably the most important one I was ever able to answer for myself. It meant I could understand the process from the examiners side.

Once a Trade Mark application is submitted, it is reviewed by a Trade Mark examiner who assesses the application against published guidelines (The Examination Guide) which specify the requirements and legislation that constitute an acceptable or unacceptable Trade Mark.

Examiners are highly trained and knowledgeable, and work within legal parameters and guidelines. It is important to remember each application is examined by a person, not a computer. This means there can also be some variation due to interpretation and opinion of the individual and hence there can be a level of subjectivity to the process.

In some instances the applicant will disagree with the Trade Mark examiner's thoughts and findings, but this is a subjective and an objective assessment process, which you must keep in mind at all times. An examiner is not trying to be difficult; they are trying to ensure your application meets statutory requirements. Very often they will let you know which part of your application is, or isn't, acceptable.

When designing any mark, and deciding to apply to register the mark, you must take this into account; rejections can be due to interpretation.

The Examination Guide is in the public domain, and can be searched and downloaded by anyone applying for a Trade Mark.

The Examination Guide gives very tight guidelines, and my experience is there is a high level of continuity and commonality to examinations, but research well before you make your application for all elements of the mark.

For example, if you are applying to Trade Mark your company name, check your company name meets the requirements. Ensure it has distinctiveness (and is not descriptive), and also check the name does not include any of the elements that are disallowed or protected from Trade Marking. If there are several ways to write your company name e.g. with capitals, spaces, full stops, italics etc that constitute a series mark, check all variations also. It will only take a few minutes of research to ensure you have covered all aspects, which can save considerable time when responding to any objection made due to lack of checking.

What do examiners say about how they assess Trade Mark application?

I have spoken with many UK examiners to try to find out how they begin to assess an application. One of the most helpful examiners gave me his method: when he receives a new application he looks at the mark being applied for. He does not look at the applicant's name, the classes to be registered, descriptions of goods or services or any other detail of the application. He looks at the mark, and asks himself the question: "what is this mark being used for and what products or services will it be applied to?".

He tries to guess the purpose and use of the mark. He writes it down on a piece of paper. It is his 'blind' test.

His next stage is to compare his notes to the application; in general, if the classes and descriptions for the primary use of the product or service (listed in the application) are similar to those he has noted during his 'blind' assessment, his initial conclusion is the mark is not sufficiently distinctive to be registered as a Trade Mark.

If there are some grey areas, he will then ask colleagues for their opinion too.

Tip: Before applying for a Trade Mark, conduct a similar 'blind' test yourself. Ask people who do not know your mark what they think it relates to. Their comments can give an indication of whether it is sufficiently distinctive to be registered as a Trade Mark; if they can work out what your mark relates to, then the examiner will also as it is descriptive.

The application is checked against the Examination Guide to ensure compliance and against all other registered Trade Marks within the same classes to check whether there are any identical, confusingly similar, or if there is a potential partial infringement.

A cross-search is also performed in related classes to ensure there are no registered marks covering the same or similar goods or services to the application and are registered in other corresponding classes.

The examiner uses experience and discretion when performing a cross-search across classes; there is a cross-search list they use for reference, but it is not exhaustive.

A report is created based on the examiner's research and findings, with a copy sent to the applicant by email or post.

What is in the Examination Report?

Where there are no issues or queries, the examiner's report will state the application has been accepted as the registration requirements are met. The report will state that the mark will be published in the Trade Marks Journal once the final 50% of the fees are paid (under the Right Start service).

If the examiner finds the mark being applied for is not sufficiently distinctive, is descriptive or an image that reinforces the mark, this will be clearly stated with reference to the applicable legislative requirements; the application may then be rejected.

But where there are certain issues, such as you may have selected the wrong class, or the description of the goods or services with a class is incorrect, then under the Right Start Service the examiner should report this and state what changes are required for the application to be accepted.

Where there could be potential conflicts with current registered marks, these earlier marks will be listed in the report. The mark, the holder of the mark, the classes and the descriptions will be included. Be prepared for earlier mark holders to be listed; it is very rare to receive an examination report with no earlier marks listed. The only time I have received an examination report with no earlier marks listed was for a completely original mark: Rules of Don't®. All other examination reports I have received have included earlier mark queries.

The chances are the list will include marks you did not find during your research. Review the list and check how similar your mark is to the ones listed; some may include a word or two that is part of your mark (not all the words or entire phrase), some may be a similar logo, or a mix of both.

If you proceed with your application, the examiner is obliged to notify the holder of these marks that you have made your application. This does not automatically mean anyone with a registered earlier mark will oppose your application, but there may be those who see your application as a threat to their mark or their brand and take action.

Under the Right Start Service you may have the opportunity to call the examiner to discuss the report in more detail, and in many circumstances it is possible to gain more information from them as to the actions you need to take to ensure your application is accepted. The examiner will not guarantee acceptance of the application if you make the changes; they will instruct you to submit the form with the changes made and it will be re-examined.

The opportunity to talk with the examiner is invaluable. Do not overlook this to understand exactly what needs to be done to gain acceptance of your application. When using the Right Start Service, I always try to talk with the examiner regarding the examination report (unless of course the application is accepted). Examiners are very busy, and if I call and they are unavailable, one of their colleagues usually ask how they can help. I would politely decline their offer as I want to talk with the examiner who has sent the report because some elements of the examination process are based on experience and discretion; I want to know the reasoning from the examiner.

Amendments do not incur any additional cost when using the Right Start Service. These are made on-line when the application process is completed by paying the final 50% of the application fees.

Note: classes and descriptions cannot be completely changed during the process; a substantial change would require re-examination under a new application. Also the descriptions of the goods or services cannot be widened to be more generic, they can only be narrowed to be more specific.

Once submitted, the amended application is re-examined; if the recommendations made by the examiner are followed, it will probably be approved (if you do not follow the recommendations, it may be rejected). A new Examination Report will be sent saying your application is accepted and will be published in the Trade Mark journal.

The publication date will be sent to you, and from this date there is a two-month period during which your application is placed in the public domain enabling any third party to oppose, or consider opposing your application. If the application is not opposed, your Trade Mark will be automatically registered and you will receive your Trade Mark Certificate of registration a few weeks later.

If an opposition against your application is lodged, this two month period can be extended to three months. In either circumstance, the examiner will write to you to advise. The level of opposition is a fairly low percentage of the number of applications made.

The system within Europe for a Community Trade Mark is similar, however the timeframes are longer; the application is published in the Trade Marks journal for three months, and the overall time for registration can be more than 6 months.

There may be times where the objections raised by the examiner cannot be overcome, for example if the mark is completely descriptive or does not comply with the acceptable guidelines. In this case, or if you do not want to proceed with the application, you simply do not pay the remaining 50% of the fees under the Right Start Service and the application is then abandoned.

With a Community Trade Mark, you advise the examiner that you wish to stop the proceedings and abandon the application.

In all cases, fees are non-refundable, which is a key reason to research thoroughly and ensure the application is acceptable before you start.

WHAT HAPPENS IF I RECEIVE AN OPPOSITION TO MY TRADE MARK APPLICATION?

A Notice of Threatened Opposition officially notifies the examiner that a third party is considering opposing your Trade Mark application; it does not mean action is being taken, only that it is threatened. The Notice should give the grounds for opposition and there is no cost incurred by the opposer.

This Notice of Threatened Opposition triggers a period for discussion between parties; usually held between legal representatives, to enable any resolution to the opposition. If an agreement is met, the opposer takes no further action and the discussion period passes, the examiner will see no formal opposition has been lodged, and with no opposition the mark may be registered.

If no agreement can be reached, the opposer can then issue a formal opposition notice which can instigate a legal process to resolve the issues. The formal notice requires the opposer to pay an official fee.

If an opposition is received, you can withdraw your application or fight the opposition. Where the party making the opposition already holds a registered Trade Mark and they believe your application is confusingly similar to theirs, it can be down to you as the applicant to prove it will not be detrimental to them. This can be time consuming and expensive, with no guaranteed outcome.

If an opposition notice is received, it will be necessary to take legal advice as the opposer may also demand other legal undertakings to protect their brand.

Personally I do everything possible to avoid being in a position where I will receive an opposition to my application by thoroughly researching marks, brands, classes and descriptions because legal costs responding to, or defending against, an opposition can escalate. If the opposition eventually results in a tribunal, the losing party is liable for ALL costs which can include the other party's legal fees and any tribunal/court costs - which is reason enough to get the application right first time.

WHAT MUST I PREPARE BEFORE I APPLY?

The three most important factors that must be taken into consideration when applying for a Trade Mark are:

- Classes: List ALL the goods and/or services you want your Trade Mark to cover as you cannot add any more to the list once the examiner's report is issued, or when the second stage payment is made under the Right Start Service and the process continued. You should know the class number and the description of primary use.
- Research: check no applications or registrations exist for the same or similar Trade Mark for similar products or services.
- Device: ensure the Trade Mark is right first time as it cannot be amended or changed after the application has been submitted. Check for spelling mistakes!

CLASSES

I must repeat this point as it is the most crucial element in my mind when registering a Trade Mark:

YOU CANNOT ADD ANY MORE CLASSES
FOR YOUR PRODUCTS OR SERVICE
ONCE THE TRADE MARK IS REGISTERED

Think about all possible future uses. For example, one web directory I own has a very strong brand which could be used in the computer games industry or as a mobile phone app.

When I registered the Trade Mark as a web directory in Class 35: Business Information (Provision of-); Computerised business information services, I also registered for computer games at the same time in Class 09: Computer software, software for mobile phones.

I have not created the game yet, but I know I have the protection if needed as extra classes cannot be added to the same registration once the examiner's report is issued and the process continued.

WHAT DO I NEED TO RESEARCH?

Before starting your application for your Trade Mark, you need to do research. Getting the research right is probably the most important part of Trade Marking.

Research takes time and focus and you must not skimp on this part of the process. It is the most time consuming but must be done well - you do not want a Trade Mark registration application refused because you had not researched and did not know there was already someone out there who has a Trade Mark in place.

Even though the research may seem exhaustive it is not conclusive. Only the examiner will be able to fully define whether a conflicting Trade Mark exists.

SOURCES TO RESEARCH

The main sources I research are:

- Competitors
- Register of company names
- Domain names
- Unregistered Trade Marks
- Registered Trade Marks
- Social media
- Amazon

Competitors:

I use internet research to see if anyone is out there already, who they are, how they deliver and how they promote and market. I can then check if they have any registered and unregistered Trade Marks, or if any of their suppliers have them too.

Register of company names:

I search a register of companies to see if a company name is registered which is the same or similar to the brand I intend to create.

Domain names:

I check the availability of any names for my product or service, and any competitive domains.

This is a quick search to check if any conflicting or similar domain names have been registered, are parked, or are in use.

I simply use a domain registrar to check who owns a domain name or if it is available to buy. If the domain is taken, I check the registrant's details to find out what they do.

I will also search the domain name to check for a published website. If any device is being used as a Trade Mark, it should be displayed on their website.

Unregistered Trade Marks:

There is no formal unregistered Trade Mark search, therefore using a search engine is the only option. In searching for an unregistered Trade Mark, I usually search for the mark text followed by the words 'is a Trade Mark'.

For example, if I were researching Green Pullovers, the first search I would do is for the text as written, I would then search for 'Green Pullover is a Trade Mark', I would also search for conjoined words 'Greenpullover'. If the search engine returned no conflicts, I would assume there are no unregistered Trade Marks of this type.

Even though an unregistered Trade Mark has no legal protection, there may be marks which are already known by customers and therefore could cause confusion which can be a benefit and/or a hindrance. The benefit is the mark is already well known and recognised by customers. The hindrance could be that the mark has a bad reputation or your product or service could confuse or conflict with customer expectation and therefore be detrimental to your brand.

Registered Trade Marks:

When I research for a registered Trade Mark, I search the Intellectual Property Office search website for a list of all Trade Marks. The results will include any registered Trade Marks in the UK and EU, and also those which are in the application stage.

Make sure your search includes any term that describes your product or service name, use and customer type. You need to do a thorough check to ensure there are no potential conflicts.

I research other intellectual property sites, web directories or blogs to check which brands, names, logo's etc have already been registered to ensure I do not infringe them.

Social Media:

I check out the main social media platforms and article websites for references to what I currently do and what I intend to do. This also gives me some input on the types of potential clients, the competition, who is thought to be 'a guru' in this area and the key messages and expectations people have of the product or service, including delivery, pricing and terms. Social Media immediately lets people know what is good and what is bad, so I get this insight too. If nothing is written on Social Media platforms, I ask why - is this because it is not important, not understood or no one is as yet writing about it?

Amazon:

As the Amazon platform covers so many products, I check to see if anything is available which has a similar name, brand or usage to my product or service. This is particularly useful if you offer services, to check if there are books written about your topic, who has written them and what else they do. Again it will ensure you are not encroaching on any protected marks.

There are no guarantees after all the research and preparation that you have covered everything; there could be someone or something out there you just can't find. However, researching and preparing at the front end will ensure you are positioned as best as you possibly can be for success with your application the first time round.

WHAT HAPPENS AFTER I HAVE COMPLETED MY APPLICATION?

Once you have completed the first stage of your application, you will receive notifications by email, confirming receipt of your application and your payment.

Your application enters the system and is allocated to an examiner, who assesses the application and issues an examination report.

In the UK, if your application is accepted, you will receive an email confirming this, which also requires payment of the second half of the application fees. This must be done within the stated timeframe otherwise the application may be deleted.
Personally I always pay the second fees immediately - I do not wait as this will add delays to the process.

Under the UK Right Start Service, if there are objections to your application, the examiner issues a report and you have the option to discuss and understand the grounds for objection. If the objections can be overcome through amending your application, follow the link on the examination report and state the changes being made. Your application will then be re-examined. Once the amended application is acceptable, you will receive notification; you will then need to pay the remainder of the fees.

The system for a CTM is similar, except the communication may be by email or by letter. If there are any objections raised by the examiner, you can call them to discuss and are able to make amendments if permitted under the requirements.

Your application will then be published in the Trade Mark Journal for a period of two months (UK) or three months (EU CTM), which means it is in the public domain and open for objections to be raised officially. If none are received, your Trade Mark application will be approved and the Trade Mark granted. If objections are received, you will be notified and given the opportunity to respond. In this case the publication period can be extended.

WILL I GET ANY SPAM OR UNSOLICITED MAIL ?

Unfortunately the answer to this question is a resounding Yes !

For every Trade Mark I have registered in the UK and Europe, I have received letters by post from official-looking agencies stating I should register my Trade Mark on their 'Register of Protected Trade Marks', and to do so I must pay a registration fee.

They make themselves look official by calling themselves 'Institutes', displaying EU flags and including an invoice for their Publication Proposal. These are unsolicited and are not official; the only official communications are from the IPO (Intellectual Property Office) in the UK, OHIM (the Office for Harmonization of the Internal Market; Trade Marks and Designs) in the EU or from your authorised representative.

The companies who send the letters automatically scan the Trade Mark journals; these letters usually arrive once the application is made or during the publication phase.

The letters look official as they include your details, the details of your mark and a list of all the classes.

Do not be fooled, if you read the small print it actually states these letters are not invoices, they are soliciting payment for services, and do not feel threatened or under pressure to pay to be entered on any registers. It is not a requirement, it gives no protection and offers no further benefits; it should be ignored.

If in doubt, just remember this:
The only people you have to pay any fees to is the IPO, OHIM or your representative (if you decide to use the services of a Trade Mark provider). You do not have to pay any fees to any other person or company.

I have helped many companies apply for their Trade Marks, either to register the marks on their behalf or by using our address as their contact details for correspondence. They have all received these letters from various Institutes requiring payment for inclusion in their register. Some believe they have to pay it as it is part of the registration process. In fact, one client had written their cheque for the fees as it was so official-looking. Luckily they called me before they sent the payment so we were able to stop it.

How do I use my registered Trade Mark?

To keep a registered Trade Mark in force, it must be renewed every 10 years.

You also need to use it and highlight it is a registered Trade Mark.

Once registered, you have up to five years to use your Trade Mark; you do not have to use it straight away. If you do not use it during this time, or you stop using it for an uninterrupted period of five years or more, anyone can apply to have your registration revoked on the grounds of non-use and the Trade Mark removed from the register. Having gone through the effort of registering my mark, I always use it immediately.

Even if my Trade Mark is only for printed media, I always display it in the public domain so I can prove usage.

Draw attention to your mark. Make a statement that you own the Trade Mark. The standard text is to state:

> Rules of Don't® is a Registered Trade Mark of GJ International Ltd

I use this type of statement at the footer of our web page, on any printed matter, downloadable material etc. It also distinguishes the mark from, and associates it with, my company name.

You should use your Mark, even if it is 'parked' to a later time. The more places your mark is displayed, the higher the perceived and acquired goodwill.

Your mark should be used consistently; do not vary the style or appearance, do not pluralise or hyphenate your mark; ensure you use the correct colours or styles as stated in your registration.

Do not use your Trade Mark in a way that could be confusing or misleading. This could result in your registration being revoked.

It is possible to lose the rights of your Trade Mark if the mark becomes a generic name for the products or services, but for small and medium size businesses this is almost impossible. The examples usually sited are for words such as 'escalator' which, as previously explained, was a registered Trade Mark but has become a common name (noun) for the product type. If this happens, it is almost impossible to regain the rights of your Trade Mark.

LICENSING YOUR TRADE MARK

Use of your Trade Mark can be licensed to a third party; they pay you for using your registered mark.

The difficulty with any licensing agreement is monitoring and controlling how and where the Trade Mark is used, and how often. If you do go down this route, firstly consider when and how you will allow your mark to be used, and how you will monitor this. Will the licensee pay a one-off fee for using your Trade Mark, or will the fee be for each and every use? You must lay down tight guidelines on ownership of your mark, and perhaps require a statement that "yourmark® is a registered Trade Mark of yourcompanyltd" is displayed with your mark in all instances.

Also consider how you will control quality in any licensing agreement; if the product or service delivered by the licensee is of poor quality, this will be detrimental to your Trade Mark. You should have the right to check quality and stop the use of your mark if it is used incorrectly or could be damaging or confusing to your brand in any way in the eyes of your customers.

Licensing the use of your Trade Mark can be an effective way to scale your business as your Mark is earning you passive income. Do not rely on a handshake and a verbal agreement; always enter into a contract if licensing your mark. Once you agree to a licensing arrangement, you must submit the appropriate forms to the IPO.

It is possible to sell or transfer the ownership of your Trade Mark. Officially this is known as 'assignment' and you must inform the IPO of this by signing and submitting the appropriate forms.

HOW DO I MONITOR MY TRADE MARK AFTER IT IS REGISTERED?

It is up to you as the Trade Mark owner to police your mark to make sure someone else does not register a mark similar to yours.

Monitoring your Trade Mark is vital. There are many commercially available services called Trade Mark Watch services that will automatically do this for you; all do a similar thing but pricing varies enormously.

There is one measure you should take and that is to set up a Google Alert. A Google Alert allows you to set keywords, and whenever they are listed on the internet, Google will automatically alert you to this. You can do this for your company name, product name, Trade Marks (registered and unregistered), in fact for anything that can negatively impact your business. It may also be relevant to set up an alert for marks which could be confusingly similar to yours. A Google Alert is particularly useful if someone unknowingly uses your Trade Mark, especially as an unregistered Trade Mark.

What happens if someone tries to register a Trade Mark similar to mine?

If you have a registered Trade Mark, and an application is made to register a Trade Mark similar to yours, the examiner will check the mark and if the similarity between the marks is liable to cause confusion with customers, the examiner will write to you to let you know.

The letter will detail the mark, the classes and description and tell you the next steps you can take should you wish to oppose the application. The letter is a standard format and you need to take a practical view of the application and whether you feel it will be detrimental to you.

Where the application of the similar mark is in different classes to yours, you may not be advised of the application. In this instance, should you wish to register your current marks in different classes in the future by submitting a new application, you may be refused if someone else already has a similar registered Trade Mark in those classes.

You can issue a Notice of Threatened Opposition and follow the system for opposing a new application. This will probably require input from a qualified legal practitioner.

Having to oppose a new application, or receiving an opposition, runs at a low percentage of all Trade Mark applications made. Do not worry about the threat of opposition and use this as a reason not to register a Trade Mark; upfront research is the key to success and being aware of the requirements.

How do I apply for a UK Trade Mark using the Right Start Service?

The online procedure to apply to register a Trade Mark is fairly simple to follow.

Before you start the process, make sure you:

- Know the class or classes you wish to register in AND the description of the applicable goods or services you will use for each class;
- Have access to the image file on the computer you are using to perform the registration if registering a logo or stylised device as it has to be uploaded during the application process;
- Have a list ready if making an application for a series of marks;
- A payment method - credit cards are accepted.

The process for applying for a Trade Mark is a series of on-line pages, accessed from the Intellectual Property Site under the Trade Marks tab. When you use the on-line services, the process goes through a series of steps, asking various questions and for information. Each step is as follows:

Step 1: Applicant type.

Who is completing this application: the owner or an authorised person? If you are applying for your mark yourself, you are the owner and should select this button. Being the owner does not mean it has to be registered in your personal name; if you own a business and want to register your Trade

Mark in the name of your business, you are still the owner. All you do is enter the business name and contact details. Similarly, if you work for a company and apply to register the Trade Mark on behalf of that company, as you are an employee and the Mark is in your employer's name, you are still the owner.

If you are completing the application on behalf of someone else or another business, you are 'an authorised person'. For example, if a lawyer is completing the application on your behalf, this is the button they click. It is not just for legal people; it can be a representative of any kind who is not directly related to the applicant, and who has been asked, or authorised, to make the application on their behalf. In this instance, the system asks for the details of the authorised person, and for the details of the applicant. The application will show both sets of details, but the Trade Mark will be the property of the owner, not the authorised person.

Step 2: Owner details.
If this is your first Trade Mark application, you will need to enter new details. Comploto the requested information in the online form. A business address, home address or PO Box number can be used in the address section. All details entered will be in the public domain once the application is made, and you have to tick a box to agree to this.

Step 3: The Trade Mark being applied for.
This is where you enter the words or upload the image of your Trade Mark; it continues over multiple screens.

Where your mark includes words, letters or numbers (even as part of a logo image), you must enter them. The system will ask if it is part of an image or stylised; you will then upload the image file as appropriate.

If your mark does not include words, letters or numbers, you are asked to confirm this and to upload the image file.

The uploaded image is displayed and you must confirm the image is an accurate representation of your mark. The mark cannot be changed once submitted; remember if you have used an image with the letters ™ against it on your branding, this symbol must be removed from the image file before uploading.

Step 4: Single or series mark.

If the mark is a stand-alone mark, you will continue through the application. However if it is a series mark, you will need to specify the number in the series and upload or enter each mark in the series.

Step 5: Select classes of the goods or services.

The easiest and most accurate way to do this is to Select Goods and Service From an Approved List. Searching keywords that relate to your mark will return a long list of possible classes and descriptions. Go through each line and tick the box to Add Term to your list. Once you have clicked all the classes and descriptions that apply to your mark, Confirm them and the list of selected classes and descriptions will be displayed together.

Step 6: Limitations, disclaimer and priority.

The next few steps very rarely need to be completed, and if you do not have any limitation or description, disclaimer, priority claim or if it is not a certificate or collective mark, these stages are skipped.

Step 7: Select the examination service.

The Right Start service enables interaction with the examiner if there are any areas within your application that need to be addressed during the two-stage process. If the Standard service is selected, the ability to adjust your application after examination is not possible; you will only receive a yes/no to your application with no comments or suggestions and is therefore not as flexible.

Step 8: Review application.

A summary of your application is displayed on the Next page; if it is not correct you can go through the Previous pages and adjust the information until it is correct.

Step 9: Declaration.

Once all is correct, you complete the Declaration. I always add a reference to my application for traceability.

Step 10: Payment.

The final stage is to pay the fees; these are calculated automatically.

The most important point to consider is accuracy. Any mistakes made during the registration process, especially with the mark being registered, cannot be amended once the application is submitted; you would need to start a new application.

HOW DO I APPLY FOR AN EU-WIDE COMMUNITY TRADE MARK?

The process of applying for a Community Trade Mark for EU-wide protection is very similar to the application process in the UK.

The on-line system is a single-page web form (as opposed to a series of web pages) with various sections that must be completed, and others that are optional. The application page can be found through a simple internet search for OHIM Trade Mark application.

The mandatory information required is the language, applicants details, details of the mark, the classes, fee payment and signature.
All other fields are optional and normally only relate to more complicated applications.

The various fields and information required are as follows:

CTM to import.

If you have a previous CTM, you can use this as a template to complete many of the fields and only change the necessary information pertaining to this application. If this is your first application, just leave it blank.

Applicant reference.

If you wish to add your own reference number, do so here. Otherwise leave it blank.

Languages.

There are 5 official languages: English, French, German, Spanish and Italian. From the drop-down boxes you must select the language your application is in, which is the 'first language'.

You must also select a second language from the list. This does not mean you will have to correspond in the second language as you will receive all correspondence in the first language unless you select otherwise.

Applicant(s) information.

If this is your first CTM application, you will need to 'Create Applicant' and enter new details.

There are three types of applicant to select from the drop-down box:

• Legal Entity: A company or organisation.
• Natural Person: An individual.
• Natural Person: Special Case: A person who is trading under their own name (e.g. Business owner).

Each applicant type will need to enter relevant details.

Representative.

If you are located outside the EU and do not have a personal or business address within the EU, you will need to apply using a Professional Representative.

There are two types of Professional Representative: A Legal Practitioner and an Employee Representative.

Not all Trade Mark lawyers are qualified to act as a Legal Practitioner as there are certain levels of competency and experience that must be proven before qualifying. If you use a Legal Practitioner, you need to engage with them before applying for your CTM.

An Employee Representative is someone who works directly for your company and is located in the EU. You must evidence the 'economic connection' between the applicant and the employee representative to be accepted.

Mark.

In this section you must give details of the mark you are applying to register. There are different types of mark and only one type can be selected:

Word mark:

A type-written mark; including letters, numbers, words, initials and keyboard symbols.

Figurative:

This is an image mark; stylised words, graphical images or a mix of both.

Three-dimensional mark:

Covers containers, packaging or a product as a three-dimensional shape.

Colour mark per se:

This is a mark that is in a specific colour or number of colours, of any specific shape.

Sound mark:

If applying to register a particular sound, jingle etc, two files are required, a music score in standard notation (like piano music) and an audio file of how it sounds.

Other:

Any other mark not falling within the previous categories.

All marks, except for Word marks, require a file to be uploaded that gives a graphical representation of the mark, accompanied by an audio file for a sound mark.

The probability is that your application will be for an ordinary mark: a Word mark or a Figurative mark. As an example, the logo for this book is a registered CTM as a Figurative mark.

You must then describe the Elements of the Mark.

Character set of the representation of the mark:

Specify the language it is written in.

Representation of mark:

For Word marks, enter the text, for image marks, attach the file.

Verbal element of the mark:

If your image mark contains words, numbers, symbols, letters etc, you must enter the text.

Indication of Colour(s):

If your image mark has particular colours, they must be specified.

Description of the mark:

If you wish (as it is optional), you can add a brief description of the mark.

Disclaimer:

If you are disclaiming any exclusive rights for any elements of your mark, you need to add the details (optional).

Community collective mark:

Only to be completed if you are applying for a Collective mark.

National Search.

You can request a search by Nation, which requires payment of additional fees. This is rarely necessary and is usually ignored by the majority of applicants.

Goods and Services.

This is where you select classes of the goods or services, and their descriptions. The easiest and most accurate way to do this is to Search Goods and Services from the Classification Database.

Entering keywords for searching that relate to your mark will return a long list of possible classes and descriptions. Go through each line and tick the box to Add To List. Once you have clicked all the classes and descriptions that apply to your mark, Confirm them. The list of selected classes and descriptions will be displayed together.

Priority Information, Exhibition Priority and Seniority Information.

These fields are completed if you are making a priority or seniority claim in any way and are optional.

Transformation under Madrid Protocol.

Used if you have an International Registration for a Trade Mark for the EU, and you want to transform it into a CTM. It is complicated and the probability is that if you need to do this, you will have to work with a Trade Mark lawyer or already be experienced in international Trade Marks.

Other Attachments.

Any additional information can be uploaded in support of your application.

Fees.

Select the payment method you wish to use. When paying by credit card, you will be asked to enter your card number and details once you have completed the on-line application.

Signature.

Add your details as an 'electronic signature'.

Once you have completed the on-line form, you Continue and review your application. If there are any edits you need to make, you can do so. The details may appear slightly different to the way you entered them as the system will change the format to meet regulations. In clicking Submit you complete the application and pay the fees.

TRADE MARK - RULES OF DON'T®

The opposite of what you should do isn't always what you shouldn't do. The Rules of Don't® highlight some of the issues that must be addressed or not forgotten:

Don't...

...forget that a Trade Mark can give you more credibility, professionalism and distinctiveness with your customers and your competitors.

...just think about now; think about the future. You cannot add extra products or services, or classes, to a Trade Mark once it is registered.

...think just because you are a limited company and own the Domain name that you have protection.

...think copyright is the same as Trade Mark.

...think it is expensive - Trade Mark fees are not expensive, someone plagiarising your brand can be.

...believe it is difficult - anyone can follow this system.

...rely on the letters ™ after your mark; this is unregistered and you have to prove Passing Off.

...think about going to court if you can help it, especially in Passing Off cases. It will be time consuming, expensive and will take your focus from your business.

...skimp on research - this is the most important part.

...let your Trade Mark lapse. You must use your registered mark and show it is registered by including a statement that the mark is registered, especially on websites.

WHERE DO I FIND THE WEB PAGES FOR MY ON-LINE REGISTRATION?

The following links refer to the relevant web pages for your Trade Mark application.

UK TRADE MARKS

Intellectual Property Office; Trade Marks:
http://www.ipo.gov.uk/tm.htm

Trade Mark Classification Search:
http://www.ipo.gov.uk/types/tm/t-os/t-find-class.htm

Trade Mark cross-search Classes list:
http://www.ipo.gov.uk/types/tm/t-applying/t-class/t-class-cross/t-class-cross-list.htm

Registered Trade Mark Search database:
http://www.ipo.gov.uk/tmtext

Manual of Trade Mark Practice for a copy of The Examination Guide:
http://www.ipo.gov.uk/pro-types/pro-tm/t-law/t-manual.htm

Apply online:
http://www.ipo.gov.uk/types/tm/t-os/t-os-forms/tm3-introduction.htm

COMMUNITY TRADE MARKS

Trade Marks:

http://oami.europa.eu/ows/rw/pages/ctm/index.en.do

Community Trade Mark search database:

http://oami.europa.eu/ows/rw/pages/QPLUS/databases/
searchCTM.en.do

File a CTM online:

http://oami.europa.eu/ows/rw/pages/QPLUS/forms/electronic/
fileApplicationCTM.en.do

ABOUT THE AUTHOR

Gary Jennings works with companies to help them grow globally. Known as "The Export Expert" he helps companies of all sizes to meet their international goals. He is passionate about building business for the long term, creating uniqueness and protecting and leveraging all aspects of the business. He has been in the international sector for the majority of his professional life having worked for former Fortune 500 global businesses through to his own international company.

His interest in Intellectual Property, with a focus on Trade Marks, comes from an instance where a competitor used an almost exact copy of one of his product names and he could do nothing about it. He then started to look for effective ways to protect what he creates and researched Trade Marks.

Due to changes in the way Trade Marks applications are made, it is now simple for anyone to register their own marks, without using a lawyer, whilst managing costs. This does not mean you can do everything yourself, at times the legal profession is vital, but as Gary says "you may not want to register a Trade Mark for yourself, but even if you are going to use a lawyer, you need to know this stuff anyway".

Taking a no nonsense business approach to this topic, Trade Marks Made Easy is a simple , quick and effective way to break down the jargon, understand the implications and protect what you have worked so hard in building up.

APPENDIX - LIST OF TRADE MARK CLASSES

The following section is reproduced under the terms of the UK Open Government License and is subject to Crown copyright protection (Intellectual Property Office © Crown copyright 2013).

It is included as a useful overview of the various Trade Mark classes and is general information about the types of goods and services which belong to each class. The classification system is divided between goods and services goods are in classes 1 - 34 and services are in classes 35 - 45.

Note: these lists (Class Headings) do not include all goods or services in a particular class and the on-line classification search should be used.

Goods

Class 1

Chemicals used in industry, science and photography, as well as in agriculture, horticulture and forestry; unprocessed artificial resins, unprocessed plastics; manures; fire extinguishing compositions; tempering and soldering preparations; chemical substances for preserving foodstuffs; tanning substances; adhesives used in industry; unprocessed plastics in the form of liquids, chips or granules.

Class 2

Paints, varnishes, lacquers; preservatives against rust and against deterioration of wood; colorants; mordants; raw natural resins; metals in foil and powder form for painters, decorators, printers and artists.

Class 3

Bleaching preparations and other substances for laundry use; cleaning, polishing, scouring and abrasive preparations; soaps; perfumery, essential oils, cosmetics, hair lotions; dentifrices.

Class 4

Industrial oils and greases; lubricants; dust absorbing, wetting and binding compositions; fuels and illuminants; candles and wicks for lighting; combustible fuels, electricity and scented candles.

Class 5

Pharmaceutical and veterinary preparations; sanitary preparations for medical purposes; dietetic food and substances adapted for medical or veterinary use, food for babies; dietary supplements for humans and animals; plasters, materials for dressings; material for stopping teeth, dental wax; disinfectants; preparations for destroying vermin; fungicides, herbicides.

Class 6
Common metals and their alloys; metal building materials; transportable buildings of metal; materials of metal for railway tracks; non-electric cables and wires of common metal; ironmongery, small items of metal hardware; pipes and tubes of metal; safes; goods of common metal not included in other classes; ores; unwrought and partly wrought common metals; metallic windows and doors; metallic framed conservatories.

Class 7
Machines and machine tools; motors and engines (except for land vehicles); machine coupling and transmission components (except for land vehicles); agricultural implements other than hand-operated; incubators for eggs; automatic vending machines.

Class 8
Hand tools and hand operated implements; cutlery; side arms; razors; electric razors and hair cutters.

Class 9
Scientific, nautical, surveying, photographic, cinematographic, optical, weighing, measuring, signalling, checking (supervision), life-saving and teaching apparatus and instruments; apparatus and instruments for conducting, switching, transforming, accumulating, regulating or controlling electricity; apparatus for recording, transmission or reproduction of sound or images; magnetic data carriers, recording discs; compact discs, DVDs and

other digital recording media; mechanisms for coin-operated apparatus; cash registers, calculating machines, data processing equipment, computers; computer software; fire-extinguishing apparatus.

Class 10
Surgical, medical, dental and veterinary apparatus and instruments, artificial limbs, eyes and teeth; orthopaedic articles; suture materials; sex aids; massage apparatus; supportive bandages; furniture adapted for medical use.

Class 11
Apparatus for lighting, heating, steam generating, cooking, refrigerating, drying, ventilating, water supply and sanitary purposes; air conditioning apparatus; electric kettles; gas and electric cookers; vehicle lights and vehicle air conditioning units.

Class 12
Vehicles; apparatus for locomotion by land, air or water; wheelchairs; motors and engines for land vehicles; vehicle body parts and transmissions.

Class 13
Firearms; ammunition and projectiles, explosives; fireworks.

Class 14
Precious metals and their alloys; jewellery, costume jewellery, precious stones; horological and chronometric instruments, clocks and watches.

Class 15
Musical instruments; stands and cases adapted for musical instruments.

Class 16
Paper, cardboard and goods made from these materials, not included in other classes; printed matter; bookbinding material; photographs; stationery; adhesives for stationery or household purposes; artists' materials; paint brushes; typewriters and office requisites (except furniture); instructional and teaching material (except apparatus); plastic materials for packaging (not included in other classes); printers' type; printing blocks.

Class 17
Rubber, gutta-percha, gum, asbestos, mica and goods made from these materials; plastics in extruded form for use in manufacture; semi-finished plastics materials for use in further manufacture; stopping and insulating materials; flexible non-metallic pipes.

Class 18
Leather and imitations of leather; animal skins, hides; trunks and travelling bags; handbags, rucksacks, purses; umbrellas, parasols and walking sticks; whips, harness and saddlery; clothing for animals.

Class 19
Non-metallic building materials; non-metallic rigid pipes for building; asphalt, pitch and bitumen; non-metallic transportable buildings; non-metallic monuments; non-metallic framed conservatories, doors and windows.

Class 20
Furniture, mirrors, picture frames; articles made of wood, cork, reed, cane, wicker, horn, bone, ivory, whalebone, shell, amber, mother-of-pearl, meerschaum or plastic which are not included in other classes; garden furniture; pillows and cushions.

Class 21
Household or kitchen utensils and containers; combs and sponges; brushes; brush-making materials; articles for cleaning purposes; steel wool; articles made of ceramics, glass, porcelain or earthenware which are not included in other classes; electric and non-electric toothbrushes.

Class 22
Ropes, string, nets, tents, awnings, tarpaulins, sails, sacks for transporting bulk materials; padding and stuffing materials which are not made of rubber or plastics; raw fibrous textile materials.

Class 23
Yarns and threads, for textile use.

Class 24
Textiles and textile goods; bed and table covers; travellers' rugs, textiles for making articles of clothing; duvets; covers for pillows, cushions or duvets.

Class 25
Clothing, footwear, headgear.

Class 26
Lace and embroidery, ribbons and braid; buttons, hooks and eyes, pins and needles; artificial flowers.

Class 27
Carpets, rugs, mats and matting, linoleum and other materials for covering existing floors; wall hangings (non-textile); wallpaper.

Class 28
Games and playthings; playing cards; gymnastic and sporting articles; decorations for Christmas trees; childrens' toy bicycles.

Class 29
Meat, fish, poultry and game; meat extracts; preserved, dried and cooked fruits and vegetables; jellies, jams, compotes; eggs, milk and milk products; edible oils and fats; prepared meals; soups and potato crisps.

Class 30
Coffee, tea, cocoa, sugar, rice, tapioca, sago, artificial coffee; flour and preparations made from cereals, bread, pastry and confectionery, ices; honey, treacle; yeast, baking-powder; salt, mustard; vinegar, sauces (condiments); spices; ice; sandwiches; prepared meals; pizzas, pies and pasta dishes.

Class 31
Agricultural, horticultural and forestry products; live animals; fresh fruits and vegetables, seeds, natural plants and flowers; foodstuffs for animals; malt; food and beverages for animals.

Class 32
Beers; mineral and aerated waters; non-alcoholic drinks; fruit drinks and fruit juices; syrups for making beverages; shandy, de-alcoholised drinks, non-alcoholic beers and wines.

Class 33
Alcoholic wines; spirits and liqueurs; alcopops; alcoholic cocktails.

Class 34

Tobacco; smokers' articles; matches; lighters for smokers.

Services

Class 35

Advertising; business management; business administration; office functions; electronic data storage; organisation, operation and supervision of loyalty and incentive schemes; advertising services provided via the Internet; production of television and radio advertisements; accountancy; auctioneering; trade fairs; opinion polling; data processing; provision of business information; retail services connected with the sale of [list specific goods].

Class 36

Insurance; financial services; real estate agency services; building society services; banking; stockbroking; financial services provided via the Internet; issuing of tokens of value in relation to bonus and loyalty schemes; provision of financial information.

Class 37

Building construction; repair; installation services; installation, maintenance and repair of computer hardware; painting and decorating; cleaning services.

Class 38
Telecommunications services; chat room services; portal services; e-mail services; providing user access to the Internet; radio and television broadcasting.

Class 39
Transport; packaging and storage of goods; travel arrangement; distribution of electricity; travel information; provision of car parking facilities.

Class 40
Treatment of materials; development, duplicating and printing of photographs; generation of electricity.

Class 41
Education; providing of training; entertainment; sporting and cultural activities.

Class 42
Scientific and technological services and research and design relating thereto; industrial analysis and research services; design and development of computer hardware and software; computer programming; installation, maintenance and repair of computer software; computer consultancy services; design, drawing and commissioned writing for the compilation of web sites; creating, maintaining and hosting the web sites of others; design services.

Class 43
Services for providing food and drink; temporary accommodation; restaurant, bar and catering services; provision of holiday accommodation;

booking and reservation services for restaurants and holiday accommodation; retirement home services; creche services.

Class 44
Medical services; veterinary services; hygienic and beauty care for human beings or animals; agriculture, horticulture and forestry services; dentistry services; medical analysis for the diagnosis and treatment of persons; pharmacy advice; garden design services.

Class 45
Legal services; conveyancing services; security services for the protection of property and individuals; social work services; consultancy services relating to health and safety; consultancy services relating to personal appearance; provision of personal tarot readings; dating services; funeral services and undertaking services; fire-fighting services; detective agency services.

www.ingramcontent.com/pod-product-compliance
Lightning Source LLC
Chambersburg PA
CBHW071501200326
41519CB00019B/5830